Unsafe

Ten Things About

C.S. Lewis

&

Evangelism in Narnia

Unsafe

Ten Things About

C.S. Lewis

&

Evangelism in Narnia

Reggie Weems

Unless otherwise noted, Scripture quotations are taken from The Holy Bible, English Standard Version® (ESV®) Copyright © 2001 by Crossway, a publishing ministry of Good News Publishers. All rights reserved. ESV Text Edition: 2016

ISBN 978-1-7343452-6-1

Copyright © 2020, Reggie Weems

www.10thingsabout.org

All rights reserved. No part of this book may be reproduced, scanned, or distributed in any printed or electronic form without permission.

Quotations from the following two books are used with permission:

Out of the Silent Planet by CS Lewis © copyright CS Lewis Pte Ltd 1938; *The Lion, The Witch and The Wardrobe* by CS Lewis © copyright CS Lewis Pte Ltd 1950.

Great Writing Publications
www.greatwriting.org
Taylors, SC

To buy quantities of this book at a special rate for bulk use, email info@greatwriting.org

Table of Contents

Introduction 9

1 My Claim 13

2 A Short Biography 20

3 The Natural (Christian) Writer 26

4 The Public Intellectual 32

5 Instigators and Incendiaries 39

6 How It All Began 46

7 Meanings 54

8 Why Jack Wrote The Chronicles of Narnia ... 61

9 Choosing the Fairy Tale 68

10 Evangelism in TCN 75

Conclusion 82

About the Author 84

Endnotes 85

For
Larry and Pam
Friends of Narnia

'Course he isn't safe. But he's good.
C.S. Lewis

TEN THINGS is a series of books offering biblical encouragement and practical direction on matters of concern to modern Christians who are seeking Bible-saturated, Christ-centered, Spirit-empowered, practical guidance. The series is published in an electronic and print format for quick, private, and easy access.

The books are brief and to the point, enabling readers to access immediate help and genuine hope for real-life situations. They are also written in a pastoral tone intended to shepherd hearts and minds toward Christ-centered, whole-life transformation.

This encouragement is not intended to and cannot replace personal pastoral counsel or the accountability of living transparently in Christian fellowship with other believers. Both are invaluable to you. A particular book may inspire a reader, but lifelong change only occurs in the context of Spirit-empowered living in biblical community.

Because of its biblical and simple approach, pastors may also employ the series to disciple church leaders who minister to God's flock.

Introduction

Several years ago, a close friend and schoolteacher called to express her delight in a traveling troupe that visited her school with the play, *The Lion, the Witch and the Wardrobe.*[1]

"Wonderful," I responded. "You know, that's a Christian story."

"No, it isn't," she quickly countered.

"But it is." I answered. "It was written by a thoroughly convinced Christian who wished to express his Christian worldview through a fiction retelling of the gospel."

"No. No. It isn't that at all," she steadfastly retorted.

Understanding her resoluteness, I asked, "Do you mind if I send you a couple of books—one about the author and one about the book on which the play is based?"

"I'd be happy to read them," she confidently replied.

About a month later, my dear friend once again called me to say, "You know, you are right about *TLWW*." And our conversation continued...

My friend is a brilliant, well-read, schoolteacher. But when *TLWW* visited her school, she, her fellow faculty, and students did not have the biblical framework with which to understand and interpret C.S. Lewis's most famous book, one of seven in *The Chronicles of Narnia* written specifically to retell the Christian gospel in a fictional format.

Jack, as Clive Staples preferred to be called, revealed his intent for *TCN* at the end of his book, *Out of the Silent Planet*, which was published twelve years (1938) before *TLWW* (1950), the first published book in *TCN*. The hero, Dr. Elwin Ransom, in cooperation with the unnamed narrator of the story, Lewis himself, is trying to figure out how to tell the world about the cosmic evil perpetrated by the villain, Dr. Weston. Ransom ultimately realizes that "our only chance was to publish in the form of fiction what would not be listened to as fact." This would ensure a wider reading audience than if the story was published in academic journal, science magazine, or even a newspaper. Sprinkled within the story would be "indications enough" for readers to "go farther" in their understanding of what the author meant. And then Ransom perceptively concludes: "What we need is not so much a body of belief as a body of people familiarized with certain ideas. If we could even effect in one percent of our readers a change-over from the conception of Space to the conception of Heaven, we should have made a beginning."

This is exactly what Jack has done in *TCN*. He has taken what might "not be listened to as fact" and published it "in the form of fiction." But since the 1950s when Jack wrote the series, Western civilization has shifted from a Christian mindset to a secular worldview. We are no longer a "body of people familiarized with" religious ideas. This makes *TCN* vulnerable to myriad misinterpretations.

For instance, Liam Neeson, the actor who voices Aslan in the 2005 film production of *TLWW*, stated, "Aslan symbolizes a Christ-like figure but he also symbolizes for me Mohammed, Buddha and all the great spiritual leaders and prophets over the centuries."[2] Walter

Hooper, Lewis's personal secretary, former literary trustee and now advisor to the C.S. Lewis estate responded, "Lewis would have simply denied that."[3] Hooper is right. In *TCN*, Jack retells the Bible story and intended for Aslan to represent only one person—Jesus.

TCN is a good series of books for anyone to read and enjoy. The books are good stories. But they are also unsafe. For, in them, Jack has openly hidden the most public secret and transformative truth that humanity has ever encountered: the Christian gospel. And more, he wants his readers to see it, believe it, and commit their lives to its main character. In Narnia, that someone is Aslan. In this world, it is Jesus. In *TCN*, we find a "thoroughly converted"[4] Christian, wholly committed to capturing our hearts and minds with a mythical retelling of the gospel story.

~1~

My Claim

The Chronicles of Narnia is a best-selling series of seven children's fantasy, quest novels published at a rate of about one per year between 1950 and 1956.[5] Fantasy literature is a genre of its own and normally set in an imaginary sphere, but often with characters from our world. This is true of all the *TCN* books except *The Horse and His Boy*, whose characters are not from earth. The series begins chronologically with the creation of Narnia in *The Magician's Nephew* and ends with its destruction and the discovery of true Narnia in *The Last Battle*.[6] This represents the biblical metanarrative from creation in Genesis to recreation in Revelation.

On the anniversary of his death (22 November 2013), Jack was honored with a plaque at Poet's Corner in Westminster Abbey, London. By that time, *TCN* had sold more 100 million copies in more than 47 languages. *TLWW*, the first published book of the series, has sold at least 85 million books in more than 460 editions. It is regularly recognized as one of the most popular books in the English language.

Jack believed that his books would be out of print within five years of his death, but *TCN* has been in continual print ever since its initial publication. As of August 2019, *TLWW* was voted the most popular children's fantasy novel in the United Kingdom, outpacing *The Da Vinci Code*, *Harry Potter and the Philosopher's Stone* and *Alice in Wonderland*.[7] Three movies based on TCN, and with others to come, have already garnered 1.6 billion dollars globally. It seems that Jack is more famous than ever, and his fame is exponentially increasing as an enduring cultural influence. In 2018, Netflix acquired the rights to create a new *TCN* series and films. Its 2020 drama, *Messiah*, featured a father lying next to his dying daughter reading *TLWW*.

As fantasy literature, *TCN* personalizes the cosmic battle between good and evil in the lives of children who visit Narnia. It is a well written mythical, epic quest with inherent excitement, suspense, and danger. This first or literal level makes it enjoyable and fun for children to read.

It is also said that the children who meet Aslan in Narnia return to their own worlds as better children. This makes the series very profitable and transformative on this the second, or moral level.[8]

Unbeknownst to many readers, however, *TCN* has an intended, underlying, third or anagogical level. This means it seeks to reveal the spiritual or mystical in everyday life, especially as it relates to the ultimate, divine destiny of all creation and, particularly, humans. For Jack, that means Christianity. The series is permeated with medieval themes: Irish, English, Roman, Greek mythology and, particularly, Christian theology. Its dominant character, Aslan, embodies the hero of the Bible, Jesus. This means *TCN* is a good read, but it is also unsafe, primarily because Jack intends the books serve as seven literary evangelists.

TCN isn't escapism but an invitation into true reality. Jack wrote it as fiction, a mythical story in an attempt to bypass the kind of preconceived prejudices about Christianity he held as a child and then as an atheist. He wanted to present his faith in an alternate, imaginary world that would pre-baptize the imaginations of people who might otherwise reject

Christianity from a pulpit. Through the person of Aslan, readers get to know Jesus and what it means to join his cosmic redemptive adventure of this and all worlds.

God used myth, particularly pagan myth such as the Norse sagas, to covertly and progressively awaken Jack to the personal God of Christianity. When as a seventeen-year-old atheist he first read George MacDonald's *Phantastes*, he knew there was something different about it, but he couldn't explain it. *Phantastes* didn't transport Jack into another world but transformed the way he saw and interacted with his world. It also introduced him to the power of myth as a vehicle for truth, a strategy Jack clearly applies in *TCN*.

Previous to his Christian conversion, Jack viewed Jesus as just another dying god myth—and not a very good one. But two friends, J.R.R. Tolkien and Hugo Dyson, showed him how Jesus is the true and divine myth, the end of all myths. Rather than a story created by humans as wish fulfilment, the incarnation of Jesus is myth become real in time and space. In *TCN*, Jack employs his voluminous lifetime of reading, his passion for myth, the template he gained from MacDonald, and the truth he learned from Tolkien and Dyson to engage the imagination and capture the intellect of the sincere wonderer or irreligious skeptic. Simply put, he uses fantasy to breathe truth through fiction. In *TCN*, Jack hopes for nothing less a replication of his own Christian conversion.

Jack acknowledged that most of his books were evangelistic, written for those outside of the Christian faith. *TCN* is the retelling of story of God and of every human being. Its genre may mean that children relate to it more easily than adults, but the series is intended for people of all ages. This is because he sincerely believed that every one of us will ultimately arrive at either an eternal beatific or miserific destination. *TCN* prepares us for that inescapable eternity.

Regardless of its source or intent, myth is never trivial. It is a mirror reflecting who we are, a window depicting the world we see and a lens projecting the world we desire. Myths represent our reality: what life ought to be, how it is, how we hope it can be, and what it one day will be. This is very true of Jack's myth in *TCN* and, as such, should not be taken lightly or read unreservedly. After all, what happens ultimately and eternally to those who pledge allegiance to Aslan? And what happens ultimately and eternally to those who reject him?

Think About It

Jack understood the value of a good story and the sales of *TCN* prove they are good stories, the lifetime favorites of innumerable people. But they are more than just good stories. Their real, intrinsic appeal is located in the ultimate and real story they tell: not in their first level of good storytelling or even the second level of promoting valuable morality but in that third level of telling the greatest story ever told, that of an eternal kingdom created, lost, and won by self-sacrificing love—first by its Creator and then repeatedly demonstrated by those characters who love Aslan. In effect, *TCN* subtly reminds readers that God is the love each reader is faintly haunted by, longs to experience, and forever possess.

~2~

A Short Biography

Jack's story is essential to understanding *TCN*. He was born at home in a suburb of East Belfast on 29 November 1898. His father, Albert, was a city attorney and his mother, Flora, was a Queens University honors graduate and homemaker. He inherited his rhetorical skills from his father and his logic from his mother, but none of his romantic passion from either parent.[9] His brother Warnie, who was also Jack's best and lifelong friend (and in whose arms he died), was three years older. His early life was nothing less than idyllic.

Jack was always gladly, proudly Irish and the island's influence on his imagination is inestimable. He grew up in the midst of emerald green mountains, castles, rivers, and the Irish Sea, all a land of mystery and myth. Cave Hill, visible from both of his childhood homes, possesses an impressive nineteenth-century castle halfway up its slope and the profile of a sleeping giant at its top.[10] Early in his life, Jack's parents employed a nurse named Lizzie Endicott, whose storytelling passion first led him into the mystical land of Faerie. The year he turned six, the Lewis family moved into the newly constructed home called Little Lea, a city-sized house filled with an endless supply of books for Jack's voracious reading appetite. Early in life, he loved epic tales of adventure and mythological stories of supernatural worlds. The misdiagnosis of a weak chest and Ireland's wet weather often reduced young Jack's world to the little end room of an attic—a prison turned portal—where he and Warnie created imaginary worlds. His cousin remembers young Jack sitting in a Narnian-like wardrobe built by their grandfather, enthralling her and Warnie with adventurous tales.

Three early and pivotal childhood experiences—a memory, a book, and a poem—temporarily swept Jack away into supernatural regions that gave him a lifelong desire for the Joy he felt in those fleeting incidents.[11] Everything else in his life became secondary, and he wanted to reexperience that feeling more than anything else in the world. Jack states in his autobiography, *Surprised by Joy*, that he cannot be understood apart from these events and how they shaped his lifelong pursuit of invisible, supernatural worlds beyond this earthly realm.

But Jack's life was also shaped by early sorrow. His happy, safe world became horrifically sad and dangerous when his mother died just before he was ten. Only months later, Jack was sent away from his beloved Ireland and family to endure three English boarding schools he later portrayed as worse than anything he experienced in World War I.[12] That boyhood pain temporarily ended his search for Joy. Angry at a God he could not fathom was good, Jack became an atheist before his fourteenth birthday.

Two months after the start of World War I and two months before his sixteenth birthday (September 1914), Jack moved to the village of Great Bookham, just outside of London. There, he was privately tutored by William T. Kirkpatrick or the Great Knock, as all three Lewis men affectionately referred to him. Kirkpatrick was a former Presbyterian seminary student-turned-atheist, former tutor of his father and brother, and the most wholly logical entity

Jack had ever encountered. There, Jack flourished in every way except in regard to Christianity. He left Great Bookham (April 1917) well prepared for Oxford (except in math) where he enlisted in the British Army only two months later.[13]

Jack arrived at the front line of World War I in France on his nineteenth birthday as a second lieutenant of the First Somerset Light Infantry. The war cemented his hatred for the God who had created a world neither good nor safe.[14] But Jack was always an uncomfortable atheist, living in the conflicted worlds of romance versus reason, imagination versus reality. He was nonetheless a sincere, serious, even aggressive and argumentative nonbeliever. He would later embrace Christianity with that same private fidelity and public tenacity. He was wounded on 15 April 1918, and, as a result, discharged in December of that year.

Back at Oxford, Jack graduated with a "first" in three degrees: Honour Moderations (1920), Greats (classics and philosophy) (1922), and English Language and Literature (1923). He taught philosophy at University College, Oxford, for one year and then, at the age of twenty-six, became a tutor in English literature at

Magdalen College, also at Oxford. He taught there for twenty-nine years. For various reasons, some of which will be explained later, Jack accepted the newly created chair of Medieval and Renaissance Literature at Cambridge in 1954. He gave his inaugural lecture on his fifty-sixth birthday and taught there until he retired in 1963, the same year he died.

Jack's return to his childhood faith took a long, painful, circuitous route through many sincerely held non-Christian belief systems. But just three months before his thirty-third birthday, he became a Christian. His conversion was holistic, comprehensive, and without a sacred/secular divide, making *TCN* a natural writing expression of his faith. His former atheism facilitated his understanding of common arguments against Christianity and enabled him to foresee the potential alternatives to Christ. This is one of the reasons he became an effective Christian lay apologist and evangelist.

Think About It

Jack heard exciting stories of mythical worlds before he could read. He loved, understood, and knew what a good story is and can do. Learning to read only exacerbated the incredible difference between his other-worldly experiences and the pain he endured in his later childhood, teens, and WWI. His other-worldly experiences became all too good to be true and he did his best to deny the existence of anything beyond his material world. He even chose atheism over life in a fallen world thought to be created by a God he could not believe to be good. But God would not go away and, once a Christian, Jack had a meaningful reason to write. In effect, *TCN* rewrites his childhood and, in the process, Jack invites every reader to enjoy and enter into the truest story ever told.

~3~

The Natural (Christian) Writer

Writing came naturally for Jack, in part because he had read the best authors. But of the six people living in the Lewis household when the 1901 Census of Ireland was taken, only three-year-old Jack could not read or write.[15] By the time the family moved to Little Lea, spending their first night there on Easter Sunday evening of April 1905, he could read, as well as write. His favorite childhood books included those of Beatrix Potter and her human-like animals. Before Flora died, he and Warnie reclused themselves in the little end room of their attic at Little Lea and wrote their own stories. Jack created Animal-Land and Warnie wrote stories about India.[16]

Shortly before his eighteenth birthday, Jack

took a long Sunday walk but opted to return by train to Great Bookham where he was studying with Kirkpatrick. At the platform bookstall, he purchased George MacDonald's *Phantastes*. The faire romance did not sweep him away into an imaginary realm as had happened on three early childhood occasions. Instead, it invaded his world and transformed the way he saw it. The voice that had been calling to him since childhood sat down next to him on the train in a light that Jack first called "holiness" but later understood to be Christianity. It became the strategy and template he utilizes in *TCN* as he transports children into another world for the purpose of returning them, changed and change agents, in their own world.

Kirkpatrick repeatedly wrote Albert about Jack's quick and superb mastery of Greek, Latin, German, and Italian. Mrs. Kirkpatrick also read him French novels in the evening. Jack may have completed his last degree in only one year (English Language and Literature in 1923) because he had already read every book in the course.[17] His lifelong passion for literature, education, and academic position placed him in a creative world of literary wonder and awe. Jack was an academic and scholar who provided at least five major books on English literature: *The Allegory of Love* (1936), *A Preface to "Paradise Lost,"* (1942), the third volume in the Oxford History of English Literature, titled *English History in the Sixteenth Century* (1954), *An Experiment in Criticism* (1961) and *The Discarded Image* (published posthumously in 1964).[18] Yet even in these academic works, Jack recognized the continuity between what he believed and what he wrote.[19]

But before all of that, Jack published *Spirits in Bondage* (1919) and *Dymer* (1926). *Spirits in Bondage* is a book of poetry that diatribes against God. *Dymer* is a narrative poem that presents faith as an illusory temptation. Interestingly, even Jack's pre-Christian books were motivated by and inundated with thoughts of God and faith. But the difference in his Christian fiction writing was the reason *for* his writing. Authors like George MacDonald, G.K. Chesterton, and Charles Williams opened his eyes to the power of storytelling as a worldview medium. Thereafter, Jack saw art as "an avenue to the divine [that] gave his imaginative work the possibility of playing a salvific role in readers' lives, as George MacDonald's *Phantastes* had in his own."[20]

Less than one year after his Christian conversion, Jack wrote *The Pilgrim's Regress: An Allegorical Apology for Christianity, Reason, and Romanticism*.[21] *Regress* is an imaginative, spiritual autobiography, revealing, explaining, and defending his new faith. It is also a preview of *TCN*. But just before he began writing *TCN* in earnest, he and Tolkien challenged each other to write the kind of books they liked to read. For Jack, the immediate result was *Out of the Silent Planet* (1938), the first of the (outer space) Ransom Trilogy—an anti-scientism, anti-evolution, deeply spiritual, fiction romance in which Jack retells the story of creation, the Fall, and redemption. Although Jack was perturbed when the publisher revealed its Christian premise on the dust jacket, he was also surprised when only two out of sixty reviewers recognized the Christian motif of the book. It caused Jack to lament England's profound ignorance about Christianity but to think that he could easily present the gospel as fairy romance.

After the incredible success of *Mere Christianity* (1952), many people wanted Jack to follow up with an equally strong defense and explanation of the Christian faith.[22] But Jack had already become globally famous for *The Screwtape Letters* (1942) which won him the cover of *Time Magazine* (8 September 1947). His last overt defense of Christianity occurred in *Miracles* (1947).[23]

And so it is that when, in September of 1955, Carl Henry, the founder of *Christianity Today*, asked Jack to write an article for their freshman issue, he responded that he was no longer writing direct theological works but presenting the gospel in fiction. By that time, *The Last Battle*, the final book in *TCN*, had been completed and was awaiting publication.

Think About It

Jack loved myth for all of his life. He loved stories like the Irish fairy tales his nanny told him, the human-like animals in Beatrix Potter, and the enthralling adventures of Edith Nesbit. He found a lifelong friend (Arthur Greeves) and a transforming friendship (J.R.R. Tolkien) through Norse mythology. But it wasn't until he became a Christian that Jack understand the real value of the storytelling that he experienced in *Phantastes* by George MacDonald. He assumed that he, and everyone else living in a fallen world, longed for beauty and perfection. Once a Christian, he committed himself to retelling the story—placing fact in fiction—and remythologizing the true myth that changed his life. Those stories have become Jack's most influential and enduring Christian apologetic and evangelistic tool.

~4~

The Public Intellectual

Samuel Joeckel writes that a public intellectual is someone who lives in watershed moments of social revolution, positions him or herself as an "outsider or noncomformist," possesses the means to address the masses, and can "summon the rhetorical authority to appeal to a diverse audience."[24] Jack certainly fits this definition of such a provocateur.

> His conversion to Christianity and commitment to apologetics fortuitously coincided with the rise of radio celebrity, which Lewis undeniably became as a result of his broadcast talks over the British Broadcasting Company (BBC).... His name thus established or branded, he became associated with the religious positions he defended—traditional, conserv-

ative positions that, because of the forces of secularization as well as the forces of progress, became increasingly controversial.[25]

Previous to his Christian conversion, Jack was a sincere and serious atheist. He did not hold the position lightly or thoughtlessly. There are multiple reasons why Jack embraced atheism but once an atheist, he repeatedly defended it and argued against Christianity. From his perspective, the God of Christianity deserves loathing and not worship for the painful, fallen, hostile world in which an orphaned boy had to endure breathing. He was angry at God for creating such a horrid world, but simultaneously angry at God for not existing. Even Jack later acknowledged the contradictory nature of his position. But it wasn't Christianity that made Jack an uncomfortable atheist. Jack loved myth, and his early childhood experiences of *Sehnsucht*,[26] coupled with teenage repetitions of otherworldly longings, warred with his rationalistic denials of anything supernatural or romantic. The desire for what Jack called *Joy* would not—and did not—go away. For several years, he lived in and was vexed by an internal and external world: one of romantic, otherworldly imaginings; the other rooted in the painful reality of his earthly experiences. That struggle to successfully refute the numinous made him even angrier.

Once at Oxford, Jack discovered many academic Christian friends who surprised him by their romantic rationalism. He also encountered multiple authors whose Christianity he disdained as he reluctantly read them, commenting that a young atheist needs to possess careful reading habits lest God unscrupulously sneak in through books. Once a Christian, Jack committed himself to the MacDonaldian task of publicly sharing Christ by whatever means presented themselves—in *TCN*, through romantic, mythological, epic fiction. He wrote letters, articles, and books intended to recover Britain's lost religious heritage, presided over the Oxford Socratic Club, spoke to the nation on the BBC, surrounded himself with equally devoted men, and even championed Christians for positions at Oxford. Friends who cared for him complained that he was often too explicit and aggressive, even combative in his presentations of Christianity. His overt Christianity made him a lightning rod at Oxford.

The success of *Out of the Silent Planet* led to the request from Centenary Press for a book which was part of a series introducing Christianity to non-Christians. In response, Jack wrote *The Problem of Pain (1940)*. The director of the BBC read it and, in February 1941, (during WWII) asked Jack to broadcast a series of lay talks on Christianity to the British public. The chaplain-in-chief of the Royal Air Force heard those talks and asked Jack to lecture pilots of the Royal Air Force on Christianity. "It is hard for most of us to comprehend the staggering audacity and recklessness that Lewis showed in accepting such invitations."[27] Friends warned that it would ruin him academically. In fact, Oxford elites never forgave him for publishing popular theology and speaking outside of his academic training. It costs him friendships, academic advancement, and it is one of the reasons he left Oxford for Cambridge.

But Jack is an eschatological man. Heaven and hell permeate his thinking, hence his life and livelihood. He cannot compromise on a faith of such eternal seriousness. He sincerely believes that every person is daily making choices that lead to an eventual and eternal miserific or beatific existence. The early death of his mother and the death of multiple friends in World War I impaled eternity on his heart and mind. His war experiences also introduced him to the the everyday, ordinary, non-academic Englishmen who did not understand or were uninterested in the highbrow and unintelligible preaching of clergy. Jack became a passionate translator of Christianity for them. His commitment to mere Christianity and his employment of multiple genres of communication enabled him to fulfil his primary passion of reaching the widest, most diverse population possible.[28] He regularly minimizes intramural differences within Christianity and focuses on the essential definition of Christianity and what it means to follow Jesus.

Jack became a public intellectual, an outside popularizer of Christianity and theology, a protestor, a contrarian, and a nonconformist, even a rebel, in a time when secularism became popular, even aggressive in its attempts to define reality for all humanity. And he leveraged that position to advance his fame. Such status came naturally for Jack who since childhood with Warnie had always viewed himself as an outsider in a world of "us" and "them." The death of his mother and its resulting estrangement from his father, separation from his brother, his solitary life in English boarding schools, and the losses he endured in the war prepared Jack to live on the fringe of acceptability.

His early life with Warnie and the comradery he experienced in WWI also taught him the meaning and benefit of a band of brothers in arms such as the Inklings became to him. For Jack, such rejection and isolation were simply another expression of his faith—the self-forgetfulness of losing one's life to find it. And so, in an Arthurian response of almost-mythical proportions, Jack gathered a small, countercultural collective of men who gathered weekly with the unstated but explicit purpose of defiantly overthrowing unbelief in England.

Think About It

Early in life, Jack began to look at the world through the lens of his relationship to Warnie. For much of their young lives, it was them against the world. His early banishment from Ireland and experiences in English boarding schools also prepared him for life as a Christian outlier among Oxford academicians. He rarely refused an opportunity to promote Christianity—adding to his University duties, responsibilities at home (the Kilns) and passion for writing. Speaking to the nation on the BBC expanded his ever-growing audience but simultaneously branded him as a conservative Christian in a spiritually empty world. But his experiences with death and his eschatological mindset— we are all hurtling toward an eternity of bliss or misery—motivated him to use every means at his disposal to share the gospel in myriad ways, even at great cost to himself.

~5~

Instigators and Incendiaries

Jack belonged to one of the most famous literary groups in history known as Inklings, an eclectic group of men, most of them writers and Christians. No one knows exactly how or when the Inklings began, but Jack and Tolkien were at the center of this fellowship. Jack first met Tolkien at a faculty meeting in May 1926. He was six years younger and began studying at Oxford while Tollers was serving in France.[29] By the time Jack entered the war, his new friend had already returned to England.[30]

The year after they met, Jack joined Tolkien's Coalbiters club, a reading group dedicated to learning and reading Icelandic literature in its original language.[31] Eventually, Tolkien shared with Jack a poem that he was writing, and Jack reciprocated with his own work in progress. By November of 1931, Jack had written to Arthur Greeves about his regular Monday morning meetings with his new friend. In February of 1933, he wrote again to Arthur about reading Tolkien's *The Hobbit*, which was not published until 1937.

It was in the summer of 1933 that nine friends gathered for supper at Exeter College and, afterward, a late-evening discussion in Jack's rooms. Somewhere along the line, Jack and Tolkien complained about the kind of books they enjoyed reading and challenged each other to write mythological thrillers. Tolkien intended to write something about time travel and Jack opted to write about space travel. Tolkien wrote the unpublished *The Lost Road* and began working on *The Lord of the Rings*. Jack wrote and published *Out of the Silent Planet* (1938).

Jack borrowed the name Inklings from a defunct Oxford literary society of which he and Tolkien had been members. It speaks to people who dabble in ink, people who only have an inkling of what they will say when they begin a project, and people who have an inkling of another or future world. Their Thursday-night gathering in Jack's Magdalen College rooms normally began after nine when he produced a pot of tea and asked if anyone had anything to read.

Like other normal reading clubs at that time, the Inklings were "a weekly meeting of working writers. Members brought works in progress, read them aloud, received comments and criticisms, and revised their work in response to what they heard."[32] The men influenced each other, supported one another's progress, issued challenges to each other, made real changes to one another's works, collaborated with each other and advertised each other's work.[33] Among many other books, *The Hobbit, The Lord of the Rings, Out of the Silent Planet,* and *TCN* would not exist without the Inklings as a writing collective. Those Thursday-night gatherings spilled over into Tuesday morning get-togethers where Jack's friends first saw the illustrations for *TLWW*. But the Inklings was more than just an encouraging community of writers.

When Jack invited Charles Williams to join the group, he highlighted the writing *and* the Christianity of the group. Walter Hooper states that the Inklings would not have existed without Jack's conversion, the unspoken *raison d'être* for the meetings.[34] John Wain, then a young student and non-Christian who attended the Inklings for about three years, claims the group had a powerful, clearly defined corporate mind. Most of the men were born in the late nineteenth or early twentieth century, received an Edwardian education, thought the civilized world ended in 1914, served in World War I, and returned to England with a prejudice against modernism. But Wain also wrote that the Inklings was an intentional "circle of instigators and incendiaries, meeting to urge one another on in the task of redirecting the whole current of contemporary art and life."[35]

Jack publicly and vehemently denied that assertion, claiming the Inklings was simply a gathering of friends. Jack's brother, Warnie, himself an able author and member of the Inklings, echoed his brother's sentiment. But Jack's reticence to acknowledge Wain's assertion may lie in his hatred of the kind of homogenous, exclusionary clubs that terrorized his Irish boyhood in English boarding schools. As a Christian, he longed for and delighted in surrounding himself with likeminded people. And "The Inklings originated not just from Lewis' circle of friends, but specifically from Christian friends."[36] Jack and Tolkien, around whom the group centered, as well as Williams, were each committed to a romantic Christian theology. When Jack's mother died, he compared his life to a sea of islands missing any continent. But the Inklings ensured Jack was not an island. He was part of a continent of men who held each other accountable to truth telling.

The idea that literature could be simply "a conversation among a small group of intimates, for art to become incomprehensible to a wider audience, was a matter of ethical failure" to Jack. Authors are divinely endowed with the moral responsibility to "become an avenue to truth."[37] The Inklings were essentially a protest community who viewed reality holistically and believed the salvation of souls could renew a society void of spirituality and aesthetically deprived. Since his conversion, Jack remained faithful to the dream of a more beautiful world—a realm that had haunted him since childhood.

As the acknowledged ringleader of the Inklings, Jack invested his Christian life in awakening others from the nightmarish world birthed by WWI and recruiting them to his much beloved kingdom of Christ. He served as a modern prophet who sought to revive storytelling as a gospel medium without the burden of normal Christian jargon but specifically intended to remind, awaken, and re-enchant a de-Christianized Britain. And he did so at great personal cost. He nonetheless became God's smuggler—the central figure and catalyst for a group of men committed to a Copernican revolution of faith in the post-war, cynical, non-supernatural, industrial Western world. *TCN* is the retelling of the gospel truth, but without the Inklings, it would not exist.

Think About It

After his conversion, Jack's primary friendships were formed by likeminded men who banded together because they saw something of mutual importance. Unlike Tollers, who tended to privatize friendships, Jack thought, "The more, the merrier." He intentionally created and maintained friendships with men who joined him in promoting the ethic of Christianity at Oxford and beyond. Thursday nights in Jack's university rooms was a serious, critical, iron-sharpening-iron, missional reading club. That fellowship spilled over into a weekly Tuesday lunchtime gathering of boisterous fellowship and raucous fun at the *Eagle and the Child*, known locally as the *Bird and Baby*. Both gatherings provided Jack with the treasured friendships he had longed for, but never possessed in childhood.

~6~

How It All Began

Jack loved to read and write anthropomorphistic fiction as a child.[38] A misdiagnosed weak chest, Ireland's inclement weather, and a natural passion for reading moved him indoors for an inordinate length of time. But Jack used those moments to imagine and create. On three separate childhood occasions, he felt miraculously swept away into other worlds only to be almost immediately returned, left with a sickening feeling for the loss. The supernatural encounter with otherworldliness repeated itself in his early teen years and again at Great Bookham. But the bitterness of life's hardships—the death of his mother, banishment from Ireland, and the cruelty of English boarding schools—won every battle against the hope of re-experiencing Joy. Even so, atheism was an unsatisfying and temporary escape. Once

Jack became a Christian, he finally had something of eternal importance to say. Pictures filled his mind and words overflowed in his heart. Writing became a natural conduit of expression—first in self-reflection and then as the representative of lay people who, like himself, longed for a beautifully perfect world.

Jack had possessed images of a faun carrying packages through the snow under a lamppost since he was about sixteen. When Hitler's potential blitzkrieg brought children into his house in 1939, he thought earnestly about using those pictures to tell a story much akin to what those children and all of England were experiencing.[39] His first draft was about four children named Ann, Martin, Rose, and Peter who had also fled London because of German air raids on the city. Dragons were afoot, and Jack wanted children to have faith and hope against evil.

Jack's intent, plan, and purpose for writing *TCN* is very plain, even though he also acknowledged that *TLWW* did not start that way. Until the first two months of 1949, when Jack had dreams about lions and Aslan entered Narnia, it wasn't a Christian story. Aslan was not even in the first completed draft. "Lewis maintained that at first there was nothing specifically Christian about the pictures he was seeing in his head but *that* element—as with Aslan, pushed its way in of its own accord."[40] Once Aslan came bounding in, everything changed. After that, Aslan becomes the only character to appear in all seven books. He is the cord that binds them all together. Jack explained it like this: the author in him chose the fairy tale form of the story but the man, C.S. Lewis, the Christian, wrote the story.[41]

Jack must have been surprised at Tolkien's response to *TLWW* when he first read it to the Inklings, but Tollers did not like it on several levels and for many different reasons. His first and primary objection was its obvious Christianity. He also thought it had been written too quickly. Jack had mental pictures of *TLWW* since he was sixteen. Initial work on the book began in September of 1939; some of it still extant although the children have different names, but no one knows how far he got with that particular version of the book. Thereafter, it seems the story languished for years.

In an essay titled, "Different Tastes in Literature" (1946), he mentions first encountering poetry like entering a new world through a wardrobe. In September of 1947 he wrote a letter saying that he had begun a children's book but had destroyed it after bad reviews from friends. In August of 1948, he told Chad Walsh that he was writing a book like E. Nesbit, the first modern children's writer, whom he had loved since childhood. It is the kind of story he loved to read as a child; it is the kind of story he wrote as a child; it is the kind of story that was meaningful to him; and it was the kind of story that transformed him.

Walter Hooper thinks Jack was dreaming of lions in February of 1949. The next month, Jack had supper with Roger Lancelyn Green and read him two chapters of *TLWW*, which Green endorsed. Green mentions that Jack had already shown the work to Tolkien, who disapproved. Nevertheless, the entire manuscript was completed that very month and published on 16 October 1950. It was all too fast for Tollers. It took him two and a half years to complete the initial manuscript for *The Hobbit*, which he lent to Jack in February of 1933 but was not published until 1937.

He also thought the book contained too many varying mythologies instead of being located in its own painstakingly created world like Middle Earth. For instance, it begins in a world of realism, passes through a wardrobe into a world of fantasy where human children meet a faun of Greek mythology, battle a witch too much like Hans Christian Andersen's Snow Queen, are saved by a talking lion who is far too apparently a Jesus figure (Christianity), and are gifted by Santa Claus to engage in an Arthurian quest.

Tollers also thought the entire series lacked coherence. This is probably true because Jack did not plan on writing any other books after *TLWW*. He also intended to return to the series and correct the inconsistencies, but died before completing that project. In spite of Tolkien's objections, Edith, his wife, sent a copy of each *TCN* book to their grandson.

Readers should also recognize that *TCN* is not an allegory in which every person, place, or thing in the book represents something else. Jack was heavily influenced by *Pilgrim's Progress* and his first Christian work, *The Pilgrim's Regress*, is allegorical. But there is not a one-to-one correlation between everything in Narnia and our world. For instance, Jadis is not meant to be Satan or the anti-Christ. And Aslan isn't Jesus. But he does represent the Jesus of our world as a Lion in Narnia because Jack imagined a world in which Jesus was a Lion. He called this style of writing *a supposa*l. What would a world look like if we suppose Narnia exists? What would sin be like in that world? How would redemption appear? What would Jesus look like if he assumed a corporeal form in Narnia? *TCN* is the answer to those questions.

"In summary, the Narniad is a seven-volume magician's book devised by Lewis to break bad enchantments and bring about re-enchantments by reawakening a longing for Aslan and Aslan's country."[42] Each of the books in *TCN* focuses on a different part of the Christian story and teaches what Jack called *mere* Christianity, from the beginning of everything until its end and new beginning. Jack uses the books to evangelize and disciple readers. In *TMN*, Aslan sings Narnia into existence but his creation is corrupted by the entrance of sin. *TLWW* demonstrates the themes of vicarious sacrifice and the world-changing power of a single, divine resurrection. *PC* is all about the restoration of true religion. *THHB* demonstrates Aslan's sovereign providence and the conversion of heathen. *TVDT* illustrates the spiritual life of the true believer. *TSC* illustrates the ongoing struggle between light and darkness. *TLB* is the apocalyptic culmination—the appearance of the anti-Christ, the final judgement, and the new creation. Fundamentally, *TCN* is Jack's Christianity, imaginatively retold as myth in the fantasy world of Narnia and all of its inhabitants.

Think About It

Jack was a reading specific words by the age of three, reading books at six years old, and almost immediately started writing his own childhood stories. Poetry was his first writing love, but he did not excel at it. A lifetime of reading, an almost photographic memory, otherworldly experiences, mental images of a faun, an umbrella, and a lamppost in the snow, Hitler's *Blitzkrieg*, children at the Kilns, dreams about lions, and MacDonald's template for mythologizing Christian truth burst onto the page before him as he retold Christianity in an exciting, mythical, cathartic world of supposal. Once completed, the story reimagines the Bible from Genesis to Revelation, the greatest story ever told, and the truest story Jack knew.

~7~

Meanings

Throughout his academic career, Jack argued that readers must surrender themselves to the author's purpose in writing in order to best appreciate and properly interpret a work. The storyteller sets the agenda for the story. Readers should let books tell their own story and should not impose their own interpretation. At the same time, the writer should exist as a window and not a picture—something to look through and along, but not something to look at.

Jack comes precariously close to violating his own mantra in *TCN* because he is many of his characters, either as the subject or object of his stories; much of Narnia is a reflection of him, his life story, and viewpoints on Christianity. In the most intense yet cathartic ways, Jack still feels his childhood throughout his adulthood.

All along that way, he sees God mysteriously, majestically working in his life. And so, in an overarching way, *TCN* espouses his Christian view of God's sovereignty and providence. But Jack thinks that all of these things make him a good fiction, children's storyteller. Before his readers, and especially children, reject the Christianity he had endured in childhood and most often associated with a cold, stained-glassed building and irrelevant, boring preaching, he wants to be sure they have actually encountered the real thing and, in particular, the real Jesus. For him, Christianity is the most exciting, satisfying, and rewarding adventure. People just need to see it in that light, as the story of stories.

> *The Chronicles of Narnia* awaken the reader to the imaginative possibilities of the gospel that have been there all along. *The Chronicles* serve as a reminder that if the gospel doesn't fill you with overwhelming awe and joy and fear and hope, you may not have really understood what the gospel says.[43]

And yet, Jack recognizes in *Out of the Silent*

Planet, placing fact in fiction may mean that only a small fraction of readers will see the story and that most readers will miss the author's deepest meaning. Laura Miller, a skeptic and award-winning author, is an example of many modern readers. She writes:

> In my early teens, I discovered what is instantly obvious to any adult reader: that the Chronicles of Narnia are filled with Christian symbolism and that *The Lion, the Witch and the Wardrobe* offers a parallel account of the Passion of Christ....So I was horrified to discover that the Chronicles of Narnia, the joy of my childhood and the cornerstone of my imaginative life, were really just the doctrines of the Church in disguise. I looked back at my favorite book and found it appallingly transfigured. Of *course*, the self-sacrifice of Aslan to compensate for the treachery of Edmund was exactly like the crucifixion of Christ to pay off the sins of mankind! How *could* I have missed that? I felt angry and humiliated because I had been fooled.[44]

But Jack did not intend to fool anyone. The concept of "undeception," being set free from blindness, is a major theme in *TCN*. He didn't try to conceal Christianity, but reveal it in the imaginative wonder and true excitement we often miss when reading the Gospels.

TCN has a first meaning as an epic quest adventure and it is an enthrallingly good story. This type of literature requires a quester, a reason or purpose, a destination, unimaginable challenges, and a return. *Beowulf,* the *Odyssey, Iliad, Sir Gawain and the Green Knight, King Arthur,* and the *Divine Comedy* are some of Jack's favorites and models of this type of epic literature. Jack read and loved them all. The initially reticent hero traditionally faces incredible odds, often supernatural forces, and even death as she or he crosses the boundaries of natural geography or space and time in an effort to complete the journey, accomplish mindboggling feats, win the prize, and return home, changed and victorious. This feat is rarely accomplished solo but in tandem with others whom the hero gathers into a team of likeminded comrades. All of this transpires in *TCN* as children and a host of other characters battle personal vices and cosmic enemies to obtain their own personal grail, while also saving their respective countries.

Jack believed in a universal, moral absolute that he called the *Tao* and that books could be used to positively influence children concerning this absolute morality. Stories enable children to witness virtues and vices play out in the lives of various fictional characters, as well as to watch the results of such choices. This made *TCN*'s second meaning important to him. The series is set in the context of everyday life: justice and injustice, danger, friendship, betrayal, temptation, pain, joy, fear, war, etc. The protagonists model a plethora of moral values: courage, heroism, honesty, kindheartedness, sympathy, truthfulness, courage, guilt, patience, and self-sacrifice. The characters also exercise vices like pride, greed, lying, blame-shifting, exclusion, betrayal, cruelty, and the lust for power. Jack had personally experienced many of the vices and internal struggles encountered by each of his characters. Stories enabled him to demonstrate the blessing of morality and help readers translate these virtues into personal behaviors while also recognizing the vices that undermine personal and cosmic shalom.

The first level—good stories—and the second—the *Tao*—were very important to Jack. These two layers of meaning ensure the stories can be read and enjoyed without any reference to Christianity. But Jack also knew there was a greater blessing than moral virtue, and a greater danger than moral vices.

This is why *TCN* also has a third layer and interpretation, one that makes the stories all the more meaningful and consequential. Jack thought he could use his own childhood passion for myth to place the Christian story in an imaginary world. This would remove the greatest story ever told from its association with a lectern, a stained-glass building, and uninvested listeners. Although Jack never considered himself a trained, professional theologian, he became a "literary evangelist."[45] Only the month before his death, he told a young correspondent that he was happy she had discovered the most important meaning to the series.[46]

Think About It

Jack first experienced Christianity at St. Mark's in his Dundela neighborhood. It is an imposing sandstone, Church of Ireland building, led by his maternal grandfather when Jack was a young boy. The icon of the church is the winged lion, its newsletter is called *The Lion* and there is a lion head on the rectory door, about Jack's height when he attended there as a child. Jack was christened there as a baby and confirmed there as a teenage atheist.

In 1933, he and Warnie dedicated a memorial window to their parents of St. Luke, St. James, and St. Mark with a lion wrapped around his shoulders. But Jack's childhood Christianity was cold, distant, and unfeeling. In *TCN*, he exchanged it for an exciting, mythical, epic he thought might capture the hearts of young readers as he used a story to introduce children to the Jesus he had never known at an early age.

~8~

Why Jack Wrote The Chronicles of Narnia

Jack lamented that, in his time, fairy tales had been relegated to the nursery. He knew the history of literature, understood that this wasn't always so, and he longed to see it otherwise. For him, any book worth reading was worth reading again and again. He wrote *TCN* primarily for children, but hoped that children would repeatedly return to it as adults.

Tolkien encouraged Jack to publish *TLWW* even though he thought its Christian motif was too obvious and that its overt Christianity would discourage readership. Even Jack's publisher feared that Narnia could damage Jack's reputation and the sale of his other fiction books.[47] Thankfully, Tolkien was right about encouraging Jack to publish the book, and wrong about the its potential success. Nonetheless, Jack's commitment to the Narnian Gospel was more than professional or financial.[48] Writing *TCN* was in synch with his life's passion to explain, defend, and advance the gospel, even at personal and professional cost. He was keenly aware that anyone who followed Christ can be unpopular. And yet Jesus possessed first claim to his life. More than once, he commented that he was hated among Oxford academics who never forgave his overt evangelistic bravado.[49]

G.K. Chesterton wrote that fairy tales enable ordinary people to see extraordinary things.[50] Jack hoped that by placing the already too familiar gospel in unfamiliar settings, people might see the truth for the first time. In effect, he became a translator of the old gospel for modern people. This was natural for Jack, since he loved myth and had lived as an atheist for many years. He employed the mythopoeia of a secondary world for the express purpose of enlightening readers about the real or primary world. As previously noted, *TCN* isn't an escape *from* reality, but *into* it. The whole point is to return to your original world, seeing it differently and engaging it in a new way because of what you've encountered in the imagined world. It is a redefinition of the gospel in fantastical terms that capture the imagination, inform the intellect about what is most real, and then challenge readers to join in the great cause of deconstructing unbelief and orchestrating a great revival of Christianity and its supreme ethic.

At its core, *TCN* is Jack "writing of the Christian story, of the salvation of humanity by God."[51] In the first book, *TLWW*, Jack lets us watch the Pevensie children wrestle with their divine destiny, face foes and overcome fears, make and lose friends, enjoy the Heavenly and endure the Hellish, ultimately sitting on the thrones at Cair Paravel, and, in so doing, setting all of Narnia right again. Yet, in the last book, *The Last Battle*, the children think that even Narnia is lost, only to discover that everything they truly loved is forever preserved for them in another world. This is ultimate Jack, expressing the hope that all he has lost in this world—his mother, father, childhood, friends and wife—are, in reality, saved and waiting for him in the real Narnia.[52] He sincerely believes that all the horrors of this life—a lost childhood, English boarding schools, the pain of World

Wars I and II, all sorrow—will be erased, forgotten, and replaced with a land of indescribable beauty and inexpressible Joy. This quest for joy is a spiritual journey he believes every child is experiencing. He wants his readers to experience how wonderfully transformed the world can be by meeting, loving, and surrendering to Aslan. By doing so, Jack hopes every reader will join Aslan's great, cause, the universal redemption of all creation.

Hitler invaded Poland on 1 September 1939 and Warren, a retired reservist, was recalled to active military duty and left immediately. Jack wrote to him the very next day to say that schoolgirls evacuated from London had arrived at the Kilns. The day after that, England declared war on Germany. It had all happened so fast. Jack had survived the horror of the Great War and feared he, too, might be recalled into service but, thankfully, served in the Home Guard in Oxford instead. Nonetheless, he realized that children were going to grow up in a world of inescapable, humanly created evil beyond their wildest imaginations.[53] Dragons were coming to life everywhere. The least he could do was to demonstrate that evil could be overcome. He wanted children, in the words of Chesterton, to grow up with chests, willing to courageously stand against and defeat the evil that resided in their own hearts and in the world.

Even as an adult, Jack lived with a childlike sense of wonder, mystery, joy, and terror. One friend wrote that for all of his adult life, Jack lived in "an almost uniquely persisting *child's* sense of glory and nightmare."[54] This is, in part, because he keenly remembered his own juvenile fears from which his childhood religion could not rescue him. He never forgot that, and it greatly influenced his adulthood both as an atheist and as a Christian. He wanted children to escape the cold, emotionless, irrelevant religion he endured as a child, and find the life-changing Christianity he discovered as an adult. Writing *TCN* during World War II, Jack knew that the greatest horror is not the atomic bomb and the greatest Joy is not contentment with this world. The greatest horror is, in fact, not knowing Jesus and the greatest joy is loving him.

We write fairy tales because God has placed eternity in our hearts (Ecclesiastes 3:11). We know we are promised the happiest of endings, even though we don't always experience one in this life or see it in this world. The greatest example of a happy ending, as well as the one cure for the ill of the world, is the resurrection of Jesus. So, Jack created an alternative fantastical world that demonstrates the universal redemption of all things through a resurrected Jesus. After all, a glorious world of peace and happiness beyond imagination really does exist. And when everything appears to be at its worst, as Jack repeatedly demonstrates throughout *TCN*, we can expect *eucatastrophe*, a word invented by Tolkien to describe the most unexpected turnaround of events in which a sudden, favorable, and the happiest of endings occurs.[55]

Think About It

TCN was simply one of many ways that Jack shared the gospel with England and the world. Whether in the Oxford Socratic Club, the BBC, from church pulpits or in Christian nonfiction like *The Problem of Pain*, Jack was passionate about sharing Jesus. He rejected the notion that fairy tales are just for children, and thought the fairy tale is the best way to express what he wanted to say. He didn't think that fairy tales like *TCN* would scare children, but rather could prepare them for the real world. For him, fairy tales provide the most faithful impression of reality (things to fear like evil and things to hope for like the supernatural), prepare readers for the real world (things like pain, sorrow, heroism, betrayal, even death), and point to an eternal, undeniable, and invincible hope (things like personal and world transformation).

~9~

Choosing the Fairy Tale

Jack was a literary man all of his life. His mother taught him to read particular words by the age of three and he never stopped reading, ultimately in English, French, German, Greek, Latin, and Italian.[56] As a child, he loved authors like Beatrix Potter, Edith Nesbit and Jonathan Swift. From the age of about six, he and Warnie wrote stories—Jack about Animal-Land and Warnie about India—filled with dressed animals living in the world of politics and war (the subjects they heard most about in the adult conversation at their home).[57] These fables were the result of the natural comradery of the brothers, their prison-turned-portal existence in the weather of Northern Ireland, Jack's isolation when Warnie was away at school, and an imaginary retreat after Flora's death.

These childhood memories and myths were important to Jack. He invested two Irish holidays (1927 and 1928) creating an *Encyclopedia of Boxoniana*, and later wrote almost eight pages about them about them in *Surprised by Joy*. During his Kirkpatrick years, Jack fell in love with poetry through the epic tale, *The Faerie Queene* by Edumund Spencer, and it forever "shaped his mental picture of what Fairy-Land is."[58] At Great Bookham, he also encountered MacDonald's *Phantastes: A Faerie Romance*, and it baptized his imagination. He intentionally ignored Spencer's Christianity and did not initially recognize it in MacDonald, but he was forever shaped by divine truth that permeated and spoke through those books.

His lifelong passion for reading enabled Jack to gain a First in English Language and Literature in one year instead of the normal three, primarily because he had already read most if not all of the required books. He was an English Language and Literature tutor at Magdalen College, Oxford, for thirty years, and then became the first Professor of Medieval and Renaissance Literature at Magdalene College, Cambridge (1954–63). Students marveled that he could quote any line from *Paradise Lost* and could complete any sentence from a book in his personal library. As a result of the library in his mind, *TCN* "contain[s] nearly one hundred echoes or allusions to myth, history, or literature."[59]

Jack writes that the first and essential element in judging any literature is to know why it was written and what it was intended to be. The fact that *TCN* didn't begin as a Christian story doesn't lessen either its literary worth or its evangelistic value. Instead, it enhances both. Jack didn't *have* to intend to tell a Christian story. He just did. His mythological passion, his academic expertise, and his Christian faith made it natural for him to do so. Jack writes out of his essential nature, and the work flowed as a result of who he is.

> Lewis's particular skill lay in teaching almost "without meaning to": he tells a "straightforward" story of children entering a fairyland and meeting all sorts of delightful creatures and exciting adventures, and before the reader even knows what has happened he has traversed the central story of the Gospel—not as a story of someone two thousand years in the

past, but as one in the immediate present of school holidays and railways stations, the recurrence of which makes the reader feel not just that the story is being brought up to date but that it is one that is happening again and again and is everlastingly contemporary.[60]

For Jack, faerie stories were simply the best way to accomplish his purposes because they are "the most natural way to convey"[61] the truth he wanted to present. As a literary historian, Jack chose wisely. "In choosing the fantasy genre, Tolkien and Lewis as well, adopted a literary form that could and did speak to a mass audience at the same time that it connected them with a long and vital tradition in British intellectual life."[62] In addition, Jack had personally experienced the influential power of faerie stories. He was very comfortable, even at home, in that genre. And he considered the gospel to be the ultimate myth come true; the world's greatest and ultimate story. It was just waiting to be retold in a style that first captivated the imagination (heart) and then captured the intellect (mind).

His literary tastes were established in childhood, and the Christian motif saturated every fiber of his being. Together, this made fairy-tales a natural and strategic fit. Childhood myths had turned his heart toward Norse mythology. Those myths turned him toward Christianity. He was convinced the myths he told in *TCN* could do the same in the hearts of children who are more open than adults to being taught truth. Their consciences are more sensitive; they are more acutely aware of their humanity and not yet cynical and hardened against conviction. In many ways that adults have forgotten, children understand the need for a rescue. This makes the heart of a child more perceptive and receptive to the storytelling of that redemption. And if children have encountered an emotionless, thoughtless caricature of Christianity, as Jack had in his childhood, fairy stories can rescue their hearts and thoughts about Jesus.

Jack uses fiction, fantasy, and faerie as a literary bridge between Christianity and readers who might otherwise consider the gospel old-fashioned, irrelevant, uninteresting, or otherwise objectionable. He did not want people to reject Christianity without ever really considering it in all its splendor, majesty, and wonder. After he published *Out of the Silent Planet*, the first book of the science fiction Ransom Trilogy, he was very surprised to see how easily Christianity could be publicly promoted in the fantastical genre. A whole new world opened up for him and his evangelistic passion. With all of the success of *TCN*, it may very well be that Jack's fantasy fiction is even more dangerously effective, i.e., unsafe, than any debate he ever won.

Think About It

Jack was introduced to fairy stories by his childhood nanny, Lizzie Endicott. The stories he loved as a child embarrassed him as a teenager, but he returned to them as an adult. Fairy stories literally changed his life. He thought any story worth reading as a child was worth re-reading as an adult, and that any good story was worth repeatedly reading. That is the power of the fairy story; it provides a happy ending in an unhappy world—an ending every person is haunted by and longs for because God has placed the happiest ending deep within our hearts. Jack wrote *TCN* to reawaken readers to God's story and to reanimate that love for Jesus who is its theme and culmination. Throughout the series, Aslan saves Narnia, right up until the last book, when he does not rescue that world but, rather, allows it to disappear in the light of the real Narnia, the true country, the Heaven, of Jesus.

~10~

Evangelism in TCN

Jack's conversion was holistic and comprehensive. He was consumed by the story. It was not just a compartmentalized aspect of his life and it affected every part of his existence. His whole person was immersed in Christianity and he bled bibline. Walter Hooper called him "the most thoroughly converted man I ever met."[63] Jesus became his sun and, like a man escaping a darkened room for the daylight, he saw everything by and through Christ.

As a Christian, Jack thought evangelism is the primary reason for every Christian's existence. His professional and personal life were both shaped by this mantra. "For those familiar with Lewis's works, it should hardly need argument that evangelism is a theme of central significance."[64] His friend Owen Barfield recalls Jack feeling that it is every Christian's responsibility to direct people to Christ.[65] Another acquaintance, Dorothy Sayers, recognized Jack's "missionary zeal" and worried about his undaunted, public fervor.[66] But he thinks that the most important business in life is winning others to Christ and that literature should serve that purpose. There were occasions, such as his inaugural lecture at Cambridge, when Jack was accused of spreading "Christian propaganda in disguise," and his fiction works were viewed as "overtly Christian propaganda."[67] It is all true. Less than six months before he died, Jack told an American interviewer that his writing purpose was evangelistic.[68]

Early in his Christianity, Jack was overt and confrontational in his gospel presentations, but at a certain point in his life, he discovered that implicit and latent presentations of the gospel are potentially more persuasive. This is why he refused the opportunity to write for *Christianity Today*. Stories became his primary medium for conveying the gospel. In *TCN*, he presents Christianity in the vernacular or popular language of the common, everyday person, and in a way that the everyday person delights in reading. Some readers may think they are escaping life by reading *TCN*, but they are actually entering into the truest reality, only to be confronted and changed by it before they close the book.

This is part of the reason why, in spite of its lack of confrontational overtness, *TCN* is as potent as any Jack's earlier unambiguous Christian efforts. All the major themes of Christian theology are present in the books: creation, sin, salvation, sacrifice, sovereignty, providence, redemption, forgiveness, reconciliation, sanctification, grace, mercy, and, of course, Jesus. To read it is to read the Bible story, coming face-to-face with Jesus in the person of Aslan. The whole point of *TCN* is to share the greatest truth Jack knew—the gospel of Jesus Christ.

After experiencing *TCN*, Jack wants his readers to say "Oh, I already know you" when they are introduced to Jesus. His plan is to baptize the imaginations of his readers just as his own imagination had been immersed in Christianity by reading George MacDonald's *Phantastes*. George Sayer, a student and friend of Jack's, writes, "His idea, as he once explained to me, was to make it easier for children to accept Christianity when they met it later in life. He hoped that they would be vaguely reminded of the somewhat similar stories that they had read and enjoyed before. 'I am aiming at a sort of pre-baptism of the child's imagination.'"[69]

Jack loved both imagination and reason with equal passion and thought that both are essential to a well-balanced Christianity. But he first experienced imagination and then reason. His imagination fell in love with myth. Then he learned that Christianity is the true myth—a story that has entered space and time, because it is the true story. So he wrote *TCN* to mirror his own experienced order: imagination and then reason. It follows the same paradigm by which he came to Christianity. It is Jack's mythological case for the Christian faith with Aslan as its star witness.

A single moment at the end of *TLWW* clearly answers the "why" of the reasoning for *TCN*. After the death of Jadis, Aslan leads the Pevensie children to Cair Paravel. Jack writes:

> The castle of Cair Paravel on its little hill towered up above them; before them were the sands, with rocks and little pools of saltwater, and seaweed, and the smell of the sea, and long miles of bluish-green waves breaking forever and

ever on the beach. And, oh, the cry of the sea gulls!

And then, the most unparalleled, intimate moment transpires between the author and his reader. Jack slowly raises his head from his paper. He places his Biro ballpoint pen on the desk. He reaches for his London-made Tetley's pipe and strikes a match, adding light to the early Spring sunshine sneaking past the dark green, World War II blankets-turned-curtains still hanging in the study. A thin tower of smoke soon begins to cascade toward the ceiling. His eyes follow it. He is lost in thought, intentionally letting the time pass. He is remembering. And he is weeping. It is a hushed, almost sacred moment. Finally, his gleaming eyes peer over his glasses and stare directly into the face of his guest sitting opposite him at his desk. Perhaps it is you. Perhaps it is me. And then, in a voice filled with never-ending childlike surprise and abiding Joy, Jack pointedly asks,

"Have you heard it? Can you remember?"

We are shocked. He is inviting us into his story, our story, *the* story. And in that moment, we bravely understand that everything he has written is for us. He has reimagined the true in an effort to reawaken our hearts to the memory of that far-off country of the "Emperor-beyond-the-Sea."

Jack earnestly believes that each of us can hear the voice of the true Narnia, Heaven. The echo may be faint or intentionally suppressed. But he writes *TCN* to reawaken his readers to the reality of that eternal Voice. It calls us from this broken, unsatisfying, hope-depleting world into the unseen but true and forever happy world of eternal fellowship with God through Jesus.

Think About It

The joy that Jesus brought into Jack's life was unquenchable and overflowing. In his early years, that passion for Christianity displayed itself as overt, public, and confrontational—a natural expression of Jack's sincere but bombastic personality. It oozed out of him from every pore of his being: heart, mind, voice, actions, etc. He was a living epistle in every sense of the word. As Jack matured, he began to depend more on the story itself than on the storyteller, himself. His argument for Christianity shifted from reason and then romance to imagination and then intellect. In the end, his fictionalized, mythological retelling of the gospel in *TCN* may be his most potent evangelistic effort. It has certainly reached his largest audience. He was always glad when readers went beyond the first and second meanings of the stories and found his ultimate purpose in writing, retelling the gospel story of Jesus.

Conclusion

Any story about Jack's stories is also a story about Jack because he is never more himself than when he is writing stories. The first book in this series, *The Man Who Made Narnia*, introduced Jack. This book reminds us about Jack's evangelistic purposes for *TCN*.

In his short work, *On Stories*, Jack compares the plot of stories to a net whose real purpose is not to catch the apparent prey but to so enthrall, even change us, that we will throw away our nets and follow the story to its real meaning. This is how Jack writes. He knows there is more to this world than what we initially perceive and structures his stories accordingly. He uses good stories with exciting plots to share a deeper meaning than is initially understood; one that can radically change us. It is Jack's great hope that we will enjoy his stories but also be changed by them. He doesn't want us to walk away from the book saying only, "It is a good story," but, "I have become a different person—a transformed person—as a result of reading this story."

But how is it that we are changed? Or better yet, in Jack's thinking, who is it that changes us? That is what the next book, *The Gospel According to Aslan*, is all about.

P.S. If you would like to talk more about Jack, e-mail me at reggieweems@gmail.com.

About the Author

REGGIE WEEMS is married to his childhood sweetheart, Teana. They share three children and ten grandchildren. He has pastored two congregations: the first for ten years and the second since 1991. He also teaches theology, Bible, and humanities at two universities and serves as a Doctor of Ministry mentor. His DMin in Pastoral Leadership and Management is from Liberty University in Lynchburg, Virginia (USA), and his PhD in Historical Theology is from the University of Babes-Bolyai in Cluj-Napoca, Romania.

www.10thingsabout.org

To buy quantities of this book at a special rate for bulk use, email
info@greatwriting.org

Endnotes

1 Hereafter, I have taken the liberty of using the title and then abbreviating *The Chronicles of Narnia* as *TCN* and each of the seven books as, *TLWW, TMN, PC, TVDT, TSC, THHB, LTB*.

2 https://www.dailymail.co.uk/tvshowbiz/article-1335586/Liam-Neeson-upsets-Narnia-fans-claiming-Aslan-Mohammed-Christ.html (Accessed February 27, 2020)

3 Mr. Hooper served as Jack's private secretary for a short time but has devoted his life to preserving and promoting Jack's works.

4 Walter Hooper in Preface of C.S. Lewis. *God in the Dock: Essays on Theology and Ethics* (Grand Rapids: William B. Eerdmans Publishing Company, 1970), 12.

5 The last book in *TCN* was completed in March 1953 when Jack was still a Fellow and tutor in English Literature at Oxford (1925-1954). He served as the first chair of Mediaeval and Renaissance Literature at Cambridge (1954-1963) when TMN and TLB were published.

6 *TLWW* was published first (1950) and *TMN* was published sixth (1955). But *TMN* is a prequel to *TLWW*.

7 https://www.dailymail.co.uk/news/article-7335205/The-Lion-Witch-Wardrobe-voted-UKs-favourite-book.html (accessed October 7, 2019).

8 The books are appreciated by many people on this second level. But what is the author's basis for and definition of morality? In *TCN*, that source is God himself who is the ultimate ethic.

9 Romance is synonymous with the imaginative or mythical. Faerie is not the world of fairies but the mythological world beyond human experience. Jack is famous for his fictional, romantic apologetics like *TCN*.

10 That sleeping giant is reportedly the inspiration for *Gulliver's Travels* by Jonathan Swift.

11 The memory was of a miniature garden on the lid of a tin that Warnie had made and brought into Jack's nursery. The poem was a few lines from Henry Wadsworth Longfellow's translation of *Drapa* by Swedish poet Esaias Tegnér. The book was Beatrix Potter's *Squirrel Nutkin*. Jack called these experiences, Joy, and his autobiography details these initial encounters with otherworldliness.

12 Boarding schools were actually normal for the era, but Jack's experiences were negatively amplified by Flora's death, separation Ireland and home, isolation from Warnie, the insanity of his first principal, his physical inability to participate in sports, and his sensitive nature. Warnie later reflected that Jack

was simply not made for English schools. (What incapacitated him in sports? Both his thumb joints closest to each hand was visible but didn't work. It was a malady he and Warnie inherited from Albert.)

13 Ironically, Kirkpatrick's commitment to consistent, logical integrity eventually help convince Jack that Christianity is true.

14 His first book of poetry, *Spirits in Bondage* (1919), railed against God.

15 The census records Albert, Flora, Warnie, and Jack as well as two servants, Martha and Sarah.

16 These stories were published posthumously and are available as *Boxen: Childhood Chronicles Before Narnia*.

17 Hal Poe suggested this thought in a talk he gave at the 2019 Inklings Fellowship at Montreat College.

18 This is in addition to the multitude of papers he wrote and now collected in the likes of *Rehabilitations* (1939), *They Asked for a Paper* (1962), *Studies in Medieval and Renaissance literature* (1966) and *Selected Literary Essays* (1969).

19 In his sermon, "Learning in War Time," Jack discusses how scholars advance God's truth and kingdom.

20 Stephanie L. Derrick. *The Fame of C.S. Lewis: A Controversialist's Reception in Britain and America* (Oxford: Oxford University Press, 2018), 27.

21 Jack wrote *Regress*, during a two-week vacation at the Belfast home of his lifelong friend, Arthur Greeves (15-29 August 1932) but it was not published until 1933.

22 An apologetic defends a point of view. A polemic attempts to undermine an opposing view. *Mere Christianity* is an apologetic and a polemic because Lewis both defends Christianity and seeks to undermine contrary positions.

23 *Mere Christianity* was based on a series of four BBC talks (two in 1941, one in 1942 and one in 1944). The first two talks were originally published as *Broadcast Talks* (1942), the third talk as *Christian Behavior* (1943) and the fourth talk as *Beyond Personality* (1944). Jack edited and added a Preface to the combined books which Geoffrey Bless published as *Mere Christianity* in 1952. Though published after, *Miracles*, *Mere Christianity* had actually been written and published as three different books before *Miracles*, making *Miracles* Jack's last overt apologetic book.

24 Samuel Joeckel. *The C.S. Lewis Phenomenon: Christianity and the Public Sphere* (Macon: Mercer University Press, 2013), 7-9.

25 Ibid., 9.

26 *Sehnsucht* is a German word interpreted as longing or desire. Jack uses it to represent his experiences of *Joy*. That desire is both painful – missing some unknown, unnamable something and living as though exiled from it – and pleasant – hoping for the realization of what alone can satisfy the human heart.

27 Janice Brown. *The Lion in the Wasteland: Fearsome Redemption in the Work of C.S. Lewis, Dorothy Sayers, and T.S. Eliot* (Kent: The Kent State University Press, 2018), 37.

28 Jack promoted mere Christianity (a term invented

by the Puritan Richard Baxter) for multiple reasons. It was his sincerely held view. He witnessed the destruction Irish religious sectarianism wreaked on his beloved island. Focusing on the central tenants of Christianity united rather than divided Christians. A mere Christianity also increased his potential audience of religious and irreligious people.

29 Tolkien was referred to as Tollers by friends.

30 After his discharge, Tolkien first worked at Oxford on the Oxford Dictionary, then at the University of Leeds from 1920-25; first as a Reader in English Language, and then, in 1924, as Professor of English.

31 Koal biters is a term that describes men huddles so closely around a winter fire that it appears they are biting the coal.

32 Diana Pavlac Glyer. *The Company They Keep: C.S. Lewis and J.R.R. Tolkien as Writers in Community* (Kent: the Kent State University Press, 2007), 9.

33 These characteristics of the Inklings are derived from *The Company They Keep* by Diana Pavlac Glyer.

34 Walter Hooper. "The Inklings," in *C.S. Lewis & His Circle: Essays and memoirs from the Oxford C.S. Lewis Society*, eds., Roger White, Judith Wolfe, Brendan N. Wolfe (Oxford: Oxford University Press, 2015), 201.

35 John Wain. *Sprightly Running: Part of an Autobiography* (New York: St. Martin's Press, 1962), 179 & 181.

36 Colin Duriez. *C.S. Lewis: A Biography of Friendship* (Oxford: Lion Hudson, 2013), 137.

37 Stephanie L. Derrick. The Fame of C.S. Lewis: A

Controversialist's Reception in Britain and America (Oxford: Oxford University Press, 2018), 26.

38 Anthropomorphism is attributing human characteristics to a deity, animal or object.

39 Four schoolgirls arrived at Jack's home in 1939 and three hundred German bombers first raided London on 7 September 1940, the first of 57 consecutive nights of bombing. It continued sporadically until May 1941.

40 Walter Hooper. *Past Watchful Dragons: The Narnian Chronicles of C.S. Lewis* (New York: Collier Books, 1979, 31.

41 ibid.

42 Paul F. Ford. Introduction, *Companion to Narnia: The Magical World of C.S. Lewis's The Chronicles of Narnia,* Revised and Expanded (New York: HarperOne, 1980, 2005), 22.

43 Jonathan Rogers. *The World According to Narnia: Christian Meaning in C.S. Lewis's Beloved Chronicles* (New York: Warner Faith, 2005), xiii.

44 An excerpt from Laura Miller. *The Magician's Book: A Skeptic's Adventures in Narnia* (Back Bay Books http://lauramiller.typepad.com/lauramiller/excerpt.html (accessed January 17, 2018)

45 Lyle W. Dorsett, *The Essential C.S. Lewis* (New York: Colliers/Macmillan, 1988), p. 8.

46 C.S. Lewis. *C.S. Lewis: Letters to Children*, Lyle W. Dorsett and Marjorie Lamp Mead, eds. (New York: MacMillan Publishing Company, 1985), 111.

47 It is ironic that modern fans can read the series without seeing any trace of Christianity.

48 Throughout his life, Jack was very philanthropic and extremely generous, to his own neglect and perhaps to a fault.

49 The September 1947 cover of *Time* magazine no doubt embarrassed many British academics with its title, 'Oxford's C.S. Lewis, His Heresy: Christianity' who, according to the article, 'is one of a growing band of heretics among modern intellectuals: an intellectual who believes in God.' Anon., 'Don v. Devil,' *Time*, 8 September 1947, 65.

50 G.K. Chesterton, "Education by Fairy Tales," *Illustrated London News*, November 18, 1905; reprinted in The Chesterton Review 28, nos. 1-2 (February/May), 9.

51 Michael Coren. *The Man Who Created Narnia: The History of C.S. Lewis* (Grand Rapids: William B. Eerdmans Publishing Company, 1994), 70.

52 Jack remained a bachelor for most of his life but married Joy Davidman Greshem, a woman led to Christ in part by Jack's writing, in a civil observance on 23 April 1956, and then again in a Christian ceremony at her hospital bedside on 21 March 1957. Joy had terminal bone cancer and died on 13 July 1960.

53 Colin Duriez has a brilliant book on this subject titled *Bedeviled: Lewis, Tolkien and the Shadow of Evil*.

54 Donald E. Glover, *C. S. Lewis and the Art of Enchantment* (Athens: Ohio UP, 1981), 34.

55 Tolkien viewed the resurrection of Jesus as the ultimate example of *eucatastrophe*.

56 The 1901 census taken 31 March notes that Jack could not read, but later that summer, Flora wrote Albert that Jack could recognize the word, 'Papa.' He was an early reader and writer.

57 These stories were posthumously compiled into a book titled *Boxen: The Imaginary World of the Young C. S. Lewis*

58 Peter J. Schakel. *The Way Into Narnia: A Reader's Guide* (Grand Rapids: William B. Eerdmans Publishing Company, 2005), 7.

59 *C.S. Lewis: The Reading Life: The Joy of Seeing New Worlds Through Others' Eyes*, ed., David C. Downing and Michael G. Maudlin (New York: HarperOne, 2019), xii-xiii.

60 C.N. Manlowe. *C.S. Lewis: His Literary Achievement* (New York: St. Martin's Press, 1987), 120.

61 Colin Duriez. *A Field Guide to Narnia* (Phoenix Mill: Sutton Publishing Limited, 2005), 84.

62 Meredith Veldman. *Fantasy, the Bomb and the Greening of Britain: Romantic Protest, 1845-1980* (Cambridge: Cambridge University Press, 1994), 38.

63 Hooper in Preface of C.S. Lewis. *God in the Dock*, 12.

64 Angus J.L. Menuge. "Introduction," *C.S. Lewis: Lightbearer in the Shadowlands: The Evangelistic Vision of C.S. Lewis*, ed., Angus J.L. Menuge (1997), 14.

65 Oral History Interview, conducted by Lyle W. Dorse., Kent, England, July 19 & 20, 1984, for the Marion E. Wade Center, p. 61. Cited in *C.S. Lewis: A Profile in Faith*, ed., Joel S. Woodruff & Thomas A.

Tarrants (Springfield: C.S. Lewis Institute, 2013), 20.

66 Dorothy Sayers, "Letter Brother George Every," 10 July 1947, in *The Letters of Dorothy L. Sayers,* vol 3, ed. Barbara Reynolds (Cambridge: The Dorothy L. Sayers Society, 1988), 314.

67 Harry Blamires, "Teaching the Universal Truth: C.S. Lewis among the Intellectuals," in *The Pilgrim's Guide:C.S. Lewis and the Art of Witness*, ed., David Mills (Grand Rapids: Eerdmans, 1988), 16.

68 "Cross-Examination," *God in the Dock,* p. 262.

69 George Sayer, *Jack: A Life of C.S. Lewis* (Wheaton: Crossway Books, 1994), 318.

www.ingramcontent.com/pod-product-compliance
Lightning Source LLC
Chambersburg PA
CBHW052109070526
44584CB00017B/2409